Dropping In On...
RUSSIA

David C. King

A Geography Series

ROURKE BOOK COMPANY, INC.
VERO BEACH, FLORIDA 32964

©1995 Rourke Book Company, Inc.

A Blackbirch Graphics book.
Series Editor: Tanya Lee Stone

Printed in the United States of America.

Library of Congress Cataloging-in-Publication Data

King, David C.
    Russia / by David C. King.
        p.   cm. — (Dropping in on)
    Includes index.
    ISBN 1-55916-086-1
    1. Russia (Federation)—Description and travel—Juvenile literature. [1. Russia (Federation)—Description and travel.] I. Title. II. Series.
        DK510.29.K55   1995
        947—dc20   94-45832
                                             CIP
                                             AC

Russia
■■■■■■■■■

Official Name: **Russian Federation**

Area: **6,592,800 square miles**

Population: **149,609,000**

Capital: **Moscow**

Largest City: **Moscow**

Highest Elevation:

Kliuchevskoi Volcano

(15,512 feet)

Official Language: **Russian**

Major Religion: **Russian Orthodox**

Money: **Ruble**

Form of Government:

Federation

Flag:

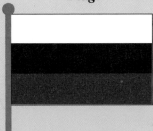

TABLE OF CONTENTS

Our Blue Ball—The Earth

The Earth can be divided into two hemispheres. The word hemisphere means "half a ball"—in this case, the ball is the Earth.

The equator is an imaginary line that runs around the middle of the Earth. It separates the Northern Hemisphere from the Southern Hemisphere. North America—where Canada, the United States, and Mexico are located—is in the Northern Hemisphere.

The Northern Hemisphere

When the North Pole is tilted toward the sun, the sun's most powerful rays strike the northern half of the Earth and less sunshine hits the Southern Hemisphere. That is when people in the Northern Hemisphere enjoy summer. When

the North Pole is tilted away from the sun, and the Southern Hemisphere receives the most sunshine, the seasons reverse. Then winter comes to the Northern Hemisphere. Seasons in the Northern Hemisphere and the Southern Hemisphere are always opposite.

8

Get Ready for Russia

Let's take a trip! Climb into your hot-air balloon and get ready to drop in on the largest country in the world. Russia stretches almost halfway across the Northern Hemisphere. It is nearly twice as large as the United States.

Russia is bordered by the Arctic Ocean in the north and by the Bering Sea and the Sea of Okhotsk in the east. The Pacific Ocean lies farther east of the Sea of Okhotsk. Large areas of the country are close to the Arctic Circle. This northern location means that winters are long and cold. There are more than 2,000 cities and large towns in Russia. Most are located in the western part of the country.

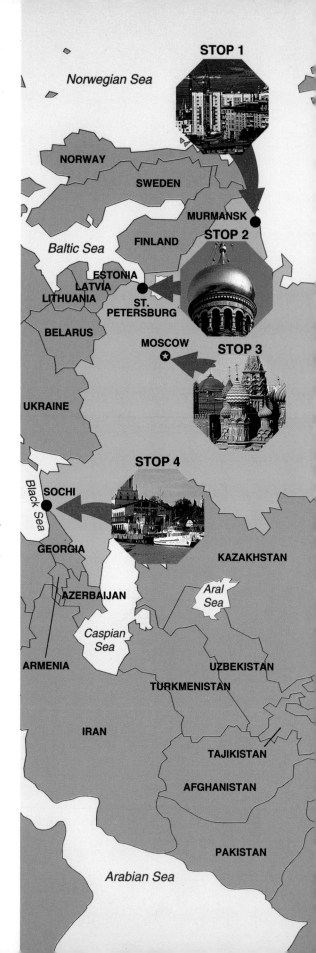

Stop 1: Murmansk

Our first stop is Murmansk. Murmansk is a city located at the northern edge of the land mass of Europe and Asia. Murmansk means "the edge of the earth." It is the world's largest city north of the Arctic Circle.

Murmansk is an important seaport because its harbor does not freeze. The fishing fleet can sail north and west to reach the Atlantic Ocean.

Because Murmansk is so close to the North Pole, summers are short and winters are very long. In winter, the Northern Hemisphere is tipped so far away from the sun that the sky remains dark

Almost one-half million people live in the fishing city and port of Murmansk.

The people of Murmansk do not mind the long, cold winters. Most enjoy winter sports.

here for almost 6 weeks. To celebrate the coming of spring, the people of Murmansk have a festival every March. This Festival of the Peoples of the North includes a cross-country ski race and a race of sleds pulled by reindeer. A swimming club called the Walrus Club has a special way of celebrating. Members chop a hole in the ice and go for a swim!

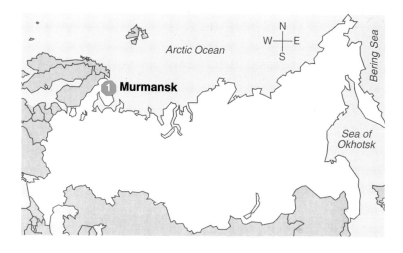

Now let's travel **southwest** to St. Petersburg.

Stop 2: St. Petersburg

St. Petersburg is built on the delta of the Neva River. The branches of the river divide St. Petersburg into 42 islands. More than 600 bridges connect the islands. St. Petersburg has 5 million people and is the second-largest city in Russia.

In summer, the Northern Hemisphere is tipped toward the sun, making the days longer. In June and July, the nights are never completely dark in St. Petersburg. Instead, there is a long, silvery twilight that the people call "White Nights."

A gold dome of St. Isaac's Cathedral shimmers in the sunlight.

St. Petersburg is famous for its beautiful buildings. Many of them are painted unusual colors, such as pale green and pink. In Palace Square, a huge granite column reaches toward the sky. The Alexander Column is the tallest single-rock column in the world. The largest building on the square is the Winter Palace, where the rulers of Russia once lived.

The most famous street in St. Petersburg is Nevsky Prospekt. The street is lined with mansions, churches, theaters, and stores. A block away, you can see St. Isaac's Cathedral.

The Hermitage Museum has one of the greatest art collections in the world.

 *Our next stop takes us **southeast** to Moscow.*

Stop 3: Moscow

Moscow is the capital of Russia and by far the largest city, with nearly 9 million people. As our hot-air balloon hovers over the city, you can see that the main streets form a series of rings, or circles. In the outer circle, there are suburbs and factories separated by large areas of forest and open fields. Many of the people live in tall apartment buildings in the middle circle.

Most tourists visit the inner ring. Here, on the banks of the Moskva River, stands a large group of buildings called the Kremlin. The Kremlin was built as a fortress more than 500 years ago. Its high, thick walls are topped by 20 towers. There are 5 gates into the Kremlin.

The inside of G.U.M. department store has a beautiful fountain.

From this angle, you can see the many magical domes of St. Basil's Cathedral and the clock tower of the Kremlin.

Arctic Ocean

N
W — E
S

Bering Sea

1
2
3 **Moscow**

Sea of
Okhotsk

Ballet is a national pastime in Russia.

Inside the Kremlin is a collection of palaces, churches, government buildings, and museums. Onion-shaped domes are part of the Square of Cathedrals. Two gigantic bell towers hold more than 50 bells. Next to the towers is the Czar Bell, weighing 200 tons, but it has never been rung. Nearby is the Czar Cannon, the largest in the world.

Outside the Kremlin walls is Red Square, a large open area used for parades and ceremonies. Facing the square, you can see the 8 domes of St. Basil's Cathedral. Each dome is a different design and color. Also facing the square is G.U.M.—a big department store with beautiful skylights and iron bridges. Moscow has more than 100 museums and many theaters, including the famous Bolshoi Opera and Ballet Theater. The city is also the center of Russia's television and movie industry. The Russian people love movies, and nearly half of the world's movie theaters are in this country.

LET'S TAKE TIME OUT

Growing Up in Russia

On the first day of each school year, Russian schoolchildren bring flowers to their teachers. The lessons on that first day are about world peace. Children go to school 6 days a week. Those who have special talents or interests can take lessons in music, ballet, or sports.

Many Russian children live in cities or large towns, and there are many things to do. Every city has a Children's Theater. The circuses are also popular, and there are many outdoor activities, such as hiking and ice skating.

These Russian children are in traditional dress.

 *For our next stop, we'll travel **southwest** to Sochi.*

Stop 4: Sochi

Sochi is a resort city that stretches for 22 miles along the coast of the Black Sea. Every year, more than 2 million Russian vacationers come to Sochi. The sunshine, mild temperatures, and warm sea water are a welcome change from the cold winters in most of Russia.

Hotels, restaurants, and campsites overlook the deep blue of the sea. Behind the city is the snow-capped Caucasus Mountain range. There are many beautiful parks along the shore and a large botanical garden. Most of the beaches here are covered with black pebbles rather than sand.

Sochi is also famous as a spa—a resort area with mineral springs, hot springs, and mud baths.

From Sochi harbor, you can take cruise ships to other ports on the Black Sea.

There are more than 50 health resorts spread around Sochi. People come from all over the world for the healthy mineral baths.

Next, we'll travel **east** to Novosibirsk.

ДОМ УЧЕНЫХ СИБИРСКОГО ОТДЕЛЕНИЯ АКАДЕМИИ НАУК СССР

Arctic Ocean

N
W—E
S

Bering Sea

1

2

3

Sea of
Okhotsk

Novosibirsk

4

5

Stop 5: Novosibirsk

To reach Novosibirsk, our hot-air balloon soars over miles of flat grassland called steppe. When we pass over hills called the Ural Mountains, we enter Siberia. Siberia is the part of Russia that is in Asia, and it reaches all the way to the Pacific Ocean. In Siberia, the land is covered with thick, dark forests called taiga.

The name Novosibirsk means "New Siberia." The city, with a population of nearly 2 million, is one of the largest in Russia. It is located on the Ob River, the fourth-longest river in the world.

Novosibirsk has a harsh climate. Summers are short, but humid and hot. In winter, temperatures often plunge to 50 degrees below zero, and the snow can be more than 4 feet deep.

Novosibirsk is an important center for industry, including steel making and gold refining. The city has modern schools, nearly 500 libraries, and a beautiful theater for opera and ballet. On the outskirts is *Akademgorodok*, which is often called Science City.

Opposite: Scientists come from all over the world to work with Russian scientists at Akademgorodok.

Outdoor Fun

Children enjoy snow sliding in Gorky Park in Moscow.

Even though the winters are long and cold, the Russian people love to be outdoors. People flock to the city parks where they can play games. One of the most popular games in Russia is chess. Many children begin to play chess at age 5.

Winter sports are popular, especially cross-country skiing. On frozen rivers and lakes, people ice skate or chop a hole in the ice for fishing. And every city has a Walrus club for people who want to take a plunge in the ice-filled water.

Many Russian boys and girls dream of becoming Olympic athletes. There are swimming pools, soccer fields, gymnasiums, and skating rinks in even small towns. Russian athletes win more medals in the Olympic Games than any other country.

Many Russian families own or rent a *dacha*—a small cottage in the country. Using the *dacha* as a base, they hike, garden, pick fruit, or swim. Meals are served outside the *dacha* and can last for hours. You might start your meal with a beet soup called *borsch*, followed by appetizers of sausage and different kinds of bread. Next, you can have *blini*—little pancakes filled with fish, melted butter, or sour cream. The main course might be a grilled fish or a special chicken dish called chicken Kiev. The long picnic supper may end with stories or singing.

There are outdoor chess tables for people to use in every Russian park.

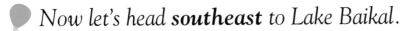 *Now let's head **southeast** to Lake Baikal.*

Stop 6: Lake Baikal

Most houses in Irkutsk have beautifully carved window frames and shutters.

Lake Baikal is one of the most amazing bodies of water on planet Earth. It is the world's oldest lake, formed more than 25 million years ago. It is also the deepest lake, more than a mile deep in some places. Lake Baikal is one of the clearest lakes, too. If you look down, you can spot a fish more

One out of every 5 drops of fresh water on our planet is in Lake Baikal.

than 100 feet below the surface of the water. In addition, there are almost 1,500 kinds of plants and animals here that are found nowhere else on Earth, including the world's only fresh-water seals.

The major city for Lake Baikal is Irkutsk. The city has tree-lined streets and many parks. In summer, the temperature in Irkutsk can be 90 degrees; but winters are very cold.

For our last stop, we'll travel **northeast** *to Khabarovsk.*

Stop 7: Khabarovsk

After leaving Lake Baikal, our hot-air balloon floats above hills and dense forests. Down below, you can see a modern train speeding toward Khabarovsk. This is the Trans-Siberian Railroad, the longest railroad in the world. It stretches nearly 6,000 miles, from Moscow to the Pacific Ocean. Traveling day and night, it takes 7 days to cross Russia.

More than 600,000 people live in Khabarovsk. It is a modern city, its streets lined with apartment buildings, stores, and restaurants. From the park overlooking the river, you can watch fishing boats bringing in their daily catch. Look downriver to the south and you see the country of China just a few miles away.

For a meal in Khabarovsk, you might try Siberian dumplings in soup, or stuffed cabbage leaves. For dessert, there is usually ice cream or *ponchiki*—hot, flat doughnuts sprinkled with powdered sugar.

The city of Khabarovsk is located on the banks of the Amur River.

Life Among the "Reindeer People"

Siberian reindeer breeders race their herd across the tundra.

In the far north of Russia, near the Arctic Circle, the climate is even colder than the places we have visited. The ground is frozen almost all year, except for a few months in the summer.

Scattered bands of people, much like the Eskimos and Aleuts of North America, live in this area called the tundra. Russians call these different groups the "Reindeer People." Most of the bands live by herding reindeer or following the wild herds. There are more than 2 million reindeer in Russia, more than in any other part of the world.

The hardy reindeer people find the tundra to be a perfect place to live. The reindeer provide them with meat, milk, and hides for warm clothing. Many of the people are nomads, moving often to follow the reindeer. Their houses, called *yaranga*, are cone-shaped tents made of reindeer hides stretched over wooden poles. The reindeer people also fish and hunt for both seals and walrus on the Arctic Ocean.

Two young Siberians prepare for a long journey on their sled pulled by reindeer.

Now it's time to steer our hot-air balloon toward home. When you return, you can look back on your wonderful adventure in Russia.

Glossary

dacha A Russian country house or cottage.

delta The place where a river divides into branches before it empties into a lake or ocean.

mountain range A row, or chain, of mountains.

nomads Members of a group or tribe that has no permanent home and travels from place to place.

spa A resort that has mineral or spring water that is good for people's health.

steppe A large, dry, flat area of grassland.

taiga An area of evergreen forests located just south of Arctic regions.

tundra An Arctic region where only low-growing plants can survive in the frozen ground.

Further Reading

Flint, David. *Russia*. Austin, TX: Raintree Steck-Vaughn, 1994.

Jacobsen, Karen. *Russian Federation*. Chicago: Childrens Press, 1994.

Kendall, Russ. *Russian Girl: Life in an Old Russian Town*. New York: Scholastic Books, 1994.

Perrin, Penelope. *Russia*. New York: Crestwood House, 1994.

Trivas, Irene. *Annie…Anya: A Month in Moscow*. New York: Orchard Books, 1992.

Note to Teachers and Librarians

For the purposes of locating each stop and teaching directional movement, we have used one projection of Russia throughout this book. Due to the extreme latitudinal expanse of Russia, however, relative directions vary with different map projections.

Index

Acknowledgments and Photo Credits
Cover and page 17: ©Wolfgang Kaehler/Liaison International; pp. 4, 6–7: National Aeronautics and Space Administration; p. 10: ©Michael Stehlik/Sovfoto/Eastfoto; pp. 11, 20, 22, 27, 28, 29: ©Sovfoto/Eastfoto; p. 12: ©Sylvain Grandadam/Photo Researchers, Inc.; pp. 13, 23: ©Sergio Penchansky/Photo Researchers, Inc.; p. 14: ©M. Bertinetti/Photo Researchers, Inc.; p. 15: ©W. Hille/Leo de Wys, Inc.; p. 16: ©Bob Krist/Leo de Wys, Inc.; pp. 18–19: ©Alex Borodulin/Leo de Wys, Inc.; p. 24 (top) : ©George Holton/Photo Researchers, Inc.; p. 24 (bottom): ©Paolo Koch/Photo Researchers, Inc.

Maps by Blackbirch Graphics, Inc.